OXFORD B

Factfiles

Animal Kingdom

RACHEL BLADON

Stage 3 (1000 headwords)

Series Editor: Rachel Bladon
Founder Factfiles Editor: Christine Lindop

OXFORD
UNIVERSITY PRESS

Great Clarendon Street, Oxford, OX2 6DP, United Kingdom

Oxford University Press is a department of the University of Oxford.
It furthers the University's objective of excellence in research, scholarship,
and education by publishing worldwide. Oxford is a registered trade
mark of Oxford University Press in the UK and in certain other countries

ISBN: 978 0 19 423674 4

A complete recording of *Animal Kingdom* is available in an audio pack ISBN: 978 0 19 423666 9

Printed in China

Word count (main text): 7,825

For more information on the Oxford Bookworms Library,
visit www.oup.com/elt/bookworms

ACKNOWLEDGEMENTS

The publisher would like to thank the following for their permission to reproduce photographs:
Alamy pp.3 (Stock Connection Blue), 14 (platypus/Natural Visions), 19 (kiwi/Jon Arnold Images
Ltd), 22 (Wildlife GmbH), 25, 35, 36–37 (Design Pics Inc.), 38 (tadpole/DP Wildlife Vertebrates),
49 (Interfoto), 62 (flatworm/Custom Life Science Images); Corbis pp iv (Jim Zuckerman),
7 (Michael & Patricia Fogden), 11 (Berthier Emmanuel/Hemis), 12 (Jim Zuckerman), 13 (Frans
Lanting), 14 (echidna/Blaine Harrington III), 15 (Frans Lanting), 16–17 (whales/Ralph Lee
Hopkins), 17 (bear/Ralph A. Clevenger), 18 (ptarmigan in snow, ptarmigan on rock/Robert &
Jean Pollock/Visuals Unlimited, Inc.), 19 (falcon/Jared Hobbs/All Canada Photos), 23 (owl/Stephen
Dalton/Minden Pictures), 24 (Tui De Roy/Minden Pictures), 28-29 (Fred Bavendam/Minden
Pictures), 30 (Stephen Frink), 31 (Paul A. Souders), 41 (Thomas Marent), 50 (Wayne Lawler/
Ecoscene), 52 (Andy Rouse), 53 (Alex Hofford/epa); Getty pp.21 (Visuals Unlimited, Inc./Gregory
Basco), 33 (cobra), 48 (Jeff Rotman), 55 (John Cancalosi), 56-57 (Steve Winter); Oxford University
Press pp.61 (turtle, geese, deer, lions), 62 (frog, falcon, fish, starfish, lion, lizard, sponge, spider,
crab, fly, centipede), 63 (a, b, c, d, f); Science Photo Library p.54 (Philippe Psaila); Shutterstock
pp.8, 26, 33 (Komodo dragon), 38 (frog), 40, 44, 45, 47, 51, 61 (camels, polar bear), 62 (earthworm,
jellyfish, octopus, algae), 63 (e).

Illustrations by: Peter Bull pp.2, 5, 6, 8, 9, 27, 43.

Picture research and illustration commissioning: Alison Wright

CONTENTS

1 Animals   1

2 How animals survive   6

3 Mammals   13

4 Birds   18

5 Fish   26

6 Reptiles   32

7 Amphibians   38

8 Invertebrates   42

9 The future   50

GLOSSARY   58

Some natural habitats   61

The animal kingdom   62

ACTIVITIES: Before reading   63

ACTIVITIES: While reading   64

ACTIVITIES: After reading   68

INDEX   73

ABOUT THE BOOKWORMS LIBRARY   76

1 Animals

The rainforest, on a hot afternoon. In the treetops, birds call to each other, and monkeys jump from branch to branch. The air is full of brightly coloured butterflies. On the rainforest floor, a snake watches a small frog, ready to catch it. And all around, hundreds of different kinds of insect are working quietly, building homes and finding food. These animals – each one so different – are all part of the animal kingdom, the most amazing group of living things in our world.

There are millions of kinds of animal in the world, and they are different in many ways. Some animals are smaller than a millimetre, but the biggest animal in the world, the blue whale, can be 30 m long. Some animals live at the bottom of the sea; others live on the world's highest mountains. Some animals live for just a day, but others can live for more than two hundred years.

Animals are made up of millions or billions of cells – tiny living things that are the smallest parts of any animal or plant. Animals are not the only living things in our world. There are other living things, for example plants, and they are made up of many cells, too. So what is different about animals? Animals are different from other living things because they can usually move around, and because they need to eat food. Plants make their own food, but animals have to find food. Then they can grow and breed.

A few minutes have passed, and the snake in the rainforest has eaten the frog. But just a few hours earlier, that same frog was having its own meal: a tasty insect that it caught in the river. That insect had just eaten, too, from the leaves on one of the trees in the rainforest. So that food has gone from the insect to the frog and on to the snake. The way food goes like this from a plant to an animal, then to another, and another, is called a 'food chain'.

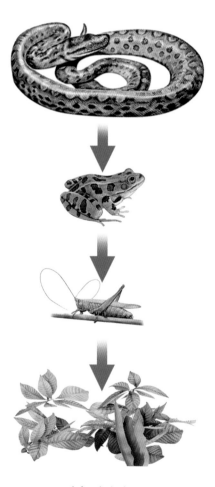

A food chain

A cheetah chasing a zebra

Some animals, like the frog and the snake, eat other animals. They are called carnivores. Many of them are predators – they have to catch other animals before they can eat them. Other animals, called herbivores, eat plants. There are also animals called omnivores which eat both animals and plants.

To help understand and study animals, scientists put them into groups. The two biggest groups are vertebrates (animals that have a backbone) and invertebrates (animals that do not have a backbone).

If someone asks you to think of an animal, you will probably think of an animal that is a vertebrate, like a dog, a bird, or a fish. That's because these animals are the ones that we see around us in the world every day. But there are many more invertebrates than vertebrates. In fact, more than 95% of all animals are invertebrates, but because many of these are tiny, we often do not see them or know about them.

Vertebrates and invertebrates are broken into smaller groups of animals. There are five main groups of vertebrates: mammals, birds, fish, reptiles, and amphibians. And there are nine main groups of invertebrates – including arthropods, cnidarians, echinoderms, and molluscs.

These groups of animals are broken into smaller groups, and the smallest group is called a species. A species is a group of animals that are the same, can breed, and have young (babies) which also breed. For example, lions are one species of big cat, and tigers are another.

Scientists know about more than one and a half million different species of animal. But every year, they find thousands of new species, and they think that there are millions more that we have not discovered yet. Who knows what is living at the bottom of the deepest seas and in parts of the rainforests where people have never been?

GROUP: vertebrates

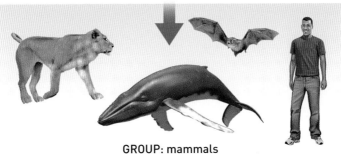

GROUP: mammals

GROUP: big cats

GROUP: lions

2 How animals survive

Something moves in the little nest at the foot of the tree. It is a baby mouse, just a few days old. She is no bigger than the end of a finger, and her eyes are still closed. But in just a few weeks, she will be fully grown. Soon, she will find a mate and have young. She will probably die before she is two years old, but her young will become adults and one day they will have babies, too. This is called a 'life cycle'.

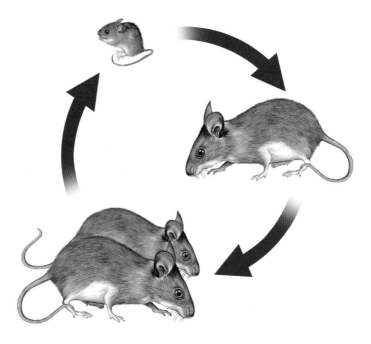

Life cycle of a mouse

The life cycle of each species is different. Almost all animals begin life in an egg. Some animals, like insects, birds, and fish, lay eggs that hatch into young, but other animals keep the eggs inside their body, and after some time, give birth to a baby animal.

When an animal is ready to breed, it needs to find a mate. But a female will not just choose any male. She needs to find the best possible mate, because she wants to have young that are strong and healthy. Many male animals find clever ways to show that they will make a good mate. Some change their colours; others do special dances or make loud noises; and some bring their females food to show that they are good hunters.

A male frog trying to find a mate

When two animals mate, the female makes eggs which are fertilized by a male. After fertilization, an egg can grow into an animal. This may take days, months, or years – a spider is born just a few days after fertilization, but an elephant after two years. Once a baby animal is born, it is ready to begin its journey to becoming an adult. For many animals, this is dangerous and difficult. So how does an animal survive?

There is a noise in the forest, and at once, everything is on the move. Birds cry loudly and fly away into the sky, and down below, animals run through the trees or up into the branches. A big predator is coming, and the animals of the forest are doing the best thing that they can to keep themselves safe: they are moving.

As the animals escape through the forest, flying, jumping, running, swimming, and pulling themselves along, they are each moving in the same way: they are contracting their muscles (making them shorter). They can do this because animal cells, unlike plant cells, can change shape.

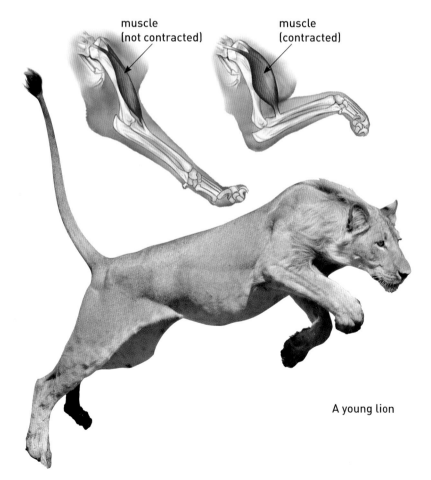

muscle (not contracted)

muscle (contracted)

A young lion

But how did the animals know that there was danger in the forest? Because of their senses – their ability to hear, see, touch, smell, and taste things in the world around them. Animals use their senses not just to stay safe from predators, but also to find food and to look for a mate.

Many animals have much better senses than people, and some have senses that we do not have at all. A snake, for example, can feel the air get warm when another animal comes near. Snakes also have a very good sense of smell, but unlike us, they do not use their noses to smell. A snake puts its long forked tongue in the air, and then moves it inside the top of its mouth, where it has something called a 'Jacobson's organ'. The Jacobson's organ tells the snake what the smell is.

Other animals also have interesting ways of using their senses. A butterfly can taste with its feet, and a bat uses sound in a very unusual way to look for prey and move around. It sends out sounds which reflect off anything that is nearby. By listening to those sounds, the bat knows which insects are near, and where they are.

A bat hunting its prey

When the predator arrived, the loud cries of birds rang through the forest. They were warning each other of danger. For all animals, communication is very important, and animals communicate with each other to stay safe. They also communicate to find a mate, get food, and care for their young.

Like us, animals use their voices and body language to communicate. But many animals also use smells, called scents. Scents can keep predators away, bring prey near, or show other animals where they are living. Many animals also use scent to show that they are ready to mate. Scientists think some female moths make a strong smell which can reach a male more than 10 km away.

The forest is quieter now. The animals were frightened by the predator, and many hurried away to their homes – places where they are safer and where they can care for their young.

Animals choose or build their homes in their natural habitat – where the temperature is not too hot or too cold for them, and where they can easily find food. Sometimes an animal's home is just a hole in a tree, or under a piece of wood, but some animals build amazing homes. The beaver bites through trees, and when the trees fall down, the beaver uses the wood to build dams on rivers. Then, in the still water behind the dam, it makes its home. A beaver's home often has water all around it, so the beaver can feel safe from predators.

The birds are flying back into the forest now, and the other animals are coming out. The predator has gone, and they are safe for now. There is time for them to find food, build their homes, or look for a mate. But trouble is never far away, and they are always looking, listening, and smelling.

So how does one species survive for a very long time? Scientists think that over many years, animals slowly change, to survive better. This is called evolution. For example, the first giraffes lived seven million years ago, and they had much shorter necks. Scientists think that the giraffes that had longer necks were able to get more food and breed more successfully. The ones with shorter necks could not get enough food and died. Over many years, the giraffe's neck slowly became longer and longer, because only long-necked giraffes stayed alive.

Because of evolution, species of animals can survive when the place where they live or the predators that hunt them change.

A beaver building its dam

A giraffe

3   Mammals

A bat flying in the night air, a whale swimming across the sea, and a monkey jumping from tree to tree – all so different, but all part of the same group of animals. They are all mammals, some of the biggest and most amazing animals in the world.

Sixty-five million years ago, mammals were small animals that had evolved from reptiles. Now they are found all around the world, on the land, in the water, and in the air. They are often intelligent, and can remember things, learn quickly, and change how they live when necessary.

Many animals leave their young soon after they are born, or even before they have hatched from the egg. But mammals often spend a lot of time caring for their young.

Cheetahs

A cheetah keeps her babies with her for sixteen to eighteen months. At first, she leaves them in dens – safe places under a tree or rock – while she goes hunting. She moves them from den to den every few days because she does not want predators to smell them. As the young get older, their mother brings them small animals that she has caught, and teaches them how to kill. The young cheetahs start to play with each other, too, chasing and fighting. Before long, they are ready to hunt.

There are three important groups of mammals – placental mammals, monotremes, and marsupials – each of which have babies in a different way.

Placental mammals give birth to young which have grown before they are born because they get food and oxygen from the placenta inside the mother's body. Many of the most important groups of placental mammals are animals that we know well. Monkeys, mice, rats, lions, dogs, whales, cheetahs, and giraffes are all examples of placental mammals.

Monotremes do not give birth to live young. They lay eggs instead. There are only two different kinds of monotreme: the platypus and the echidna.

A platypus

An echidna

A kangaroo with baby in its pouch

Marsupials are born when they are still very small, so they live on the outside of their mother's body, drinking her milk, until they have grown more. A baby kangaroo is less than three centimetres long when it is born. It moves into a big pocket called a pouch on the front of its mother's body, and lives there, drinking her milk, for several months, while it is growing. Soon, it starts to leave the pouch for a short time, and before long it is ready to live on its own.

Mammals have many features that help them to survive. First, they – unlike any other animals – make milk which they can give to their babies. Because of this, mammals do not have to look for food when they are still very young, and it is easier for them to survive. The milk that the mother makes helps to protect the baby from disease, too.

Second, mammals are the only animals which have hair. Their hair keeps them warm and dry.

Third, mammals' bodies make heat to keep them warm – they are endothermic. So a whale living in the cold Antarctic, where the temperature is very cold, still has a body temperature of around 37°C. Mammals need to eat a lot of food to keep their bodies warm. They need about ten times as much food as ectothermic animals – animals which have a body temperature the same as the temperature of the air around them. But they can survive in places that are much too cold for ectothermic animals.

Also, some mammals hibernate. If there is not enough food in the winter to keep them warm, they find a safe place and sleep for a few weeks, or even months. The animal eats a lot of food, and then, while it is hibernating, its body temperature falls, and its heart works more slowly. When the warm weather comes, it starts to move around again. Its body temperature goes up and its heart works normally again.

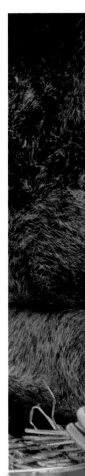

Orca whales

A bear hibernating

4   **Birds**

There are about ten thousand different species of bird in the animal kingdom. Birds, like mammals, are found in many different places all around the world. They are not the only animals that have wings – but they are different from all other animals in the animal kingdom because they have feathers.

Feathers are very important for a bird, in many different ways. The small, soft feathers that grow close to a bird's skin hold air and stop heat escaping from its body, so it stays warm. This is important because birds, like mammals, are endothermic. The longer, harder feathers on the outside of a bird's body protect it, and the bird also uses these feathers to fly.

Feathers can also be useful as camouflage – when the feathers are the same colour as the place where the bird is, they help the bird to hide. The ptarmigan, for example, has white feathers in the winter, when there is snow on the ground, and brown feathers in the summer, when it is moving around on rocks or in grass.

A ptarmigan in winter

A ptarmigan in summer

A peregrine falcon

bill

feather

A kiwi

Because birds need their feathers to survive, they take care of them, cleaning and arranging them carefully. This is called preening.

Birds evolved from reptiles millions of years ago, and as they evolved, most became very good at flying. They have strong muscles which make their wings move, and they have thin, hollow bones so their bodies are very light.

The peregrine falcon is the fastest animal in the world. It flies down through the air at more than 300 km per hour to attack.

But not all birds can fly. The New Zealand kiwi, a strange-looking bird with tiny wings and hair-like feathers, is one of about forty species of birds that do not leave the ground. Scientists think that this is because there were no mammal predators in New Zealand until people arrived there 750 years ago. The kiwi was safe living on the ground, so it did not need to fly.

All female birds lay eggs, and most birds make nests to protect their eggs from bad weather and predators. Birds usually sit on their eggs in the nest for two weeks or more to protect them and keep them warm. Then, when a baby bird is ready to hatch, it breaks out of the egg using a hard bit on its bill called an 'egg tooth'. Most baby birds cannot fly at first, so they need their parents to bring them food.

Birds do not have teeth. They catch and carry their food with a bill – so species of birds which eat different food have different shapes of bills. The peregrine falcon's bill is sharp and rounded for cutting up meat, while the toucan's long bill can easily reach fruit and insects from trees. The food is then broken down with a special organ in the birds' stomach called a gizzard, which has very powerful muscles.

For some birds, there is a long journey to make almost as soon as they can fly. Many birds nest in one part of the world in the summer, and then fly to warmer places where there is more food in the winter. This is called migration. Some birds make very long journeys when they migrate. The Arctic tern, a white seabird with a black head, flies 70,000 km around the world every year from the Arctic to the Antarctic and then back again.

There is little time to rest when a bird arrives back in its nesting ground. Male birds have to work hard to show the females that they will make a good mate. Some do this by singing, because a bird that can sing lots of different songs is intelligent and healthy.

Other birds grow brightly coloured feathers when they are ready to mate, do special dances, preen each other, or bring each other food.

A toucan

The Satin Bowerbird works extra hard to find a mate. He builds a bower – a special safe place, like a den – from grass and small branches. He works very carefully on his bower, changing it and adding bits to it every day. Then, perhaps because his own feathers are blue, he looks for blue things, for example flowers or pieces of paper, and puts these near the front of the bower.

A Satin Bowerbird

The male weaver bird is also busy at mating time. This little bird uses grasses and small branches to make beautiful nests that hang from trees. The weaver bird's nest is bigger than any other bird's nest, and is very strong. The weaver bird cleverly builds an entrance that is big enough for his mate but not big enough for any predators. But the male weaver bird's work is not easy – if a female does not think that the nest is good enough, he breaks it up and builds a new one.

Night-time. The owl seems to come from nowhere, moving silently through the air with its soft feathers. It flies quickly down towards a mouse on the ground, and before the mouse can see or hear a thing, the owl's strong feet have carried it away. The owl is a bird of prey and a highly successful night hunter. Scientists put birds into many different groups, including birds of prey, waders, passerines, and woodpeckers.

Birds of prey are very easy to recognize. They are often at the top of the food chain because they eat other vertebrates – snakes, lizards, frogs, fish, small mammals, and other birds – and are able to catch prey easily thanks to their excellent eyesight. A peregrine falcon's eyesight is eight times better than a person's, and it can see a small mouse from 3,000 m away.

A flamingo

With its long legs and neck, big bill, and colourful feathers, the flamingo looks very different from a bird of prey. The flamingo is a wader. Waders are birds that live near rivers, lakes, and other wet places where they can find lots of food. The flamingo does not eat mammals like a bird of prey. It uses its big bill to 'filter-feed' on plants and small fish: it takes lots of water in, then empties it out so only the food is left.

One of the biggest groups of birds is the passerines, which are found all around the world. Most of them are small, and they have special feet so they can stand on very small branches and even on pieces of grass. They are also well-known for the beautiful songs that they sing.

Woodpeckers make sounds of a different kind when they hit trees with their bills. They do this to make a hole in the tree for their home, and also to find insects which they then pull out with their very long, sticky tongues. A woodpecker has a very strong head. It needs this because it sometimes hits a tree with its bill several thousand times a day.

A woodpecker finding insects

5   Fish

Fish are the biggest and also the oldest group of vertebrates. From 12-metre-long sharks to tiny fish that are less than a centimetre long, these animals live in rivers, seas, and lakes.

Their long, smooth bodies can move easily through the water, and they use their fins to push themselves forward and to change direction. A covering of scales protects them and stops water getting through their skin.

Fish

Fish are ectothermic – their body temperature is the same as the temperature of the water around them. But because the temperature of seas and rivers does not change very much, fish's bodies are the same temperature most of the time.

But what about breathing? Fish can breathe in water because they have special organs called gills, which are behind their mouth on both sides of their body. The gills are full of blood, so when a fish takes in water through its mouth, the water goes over the gills, and the oxygen in it moves into the blood. Water then goes out of the fish through the gill covers.

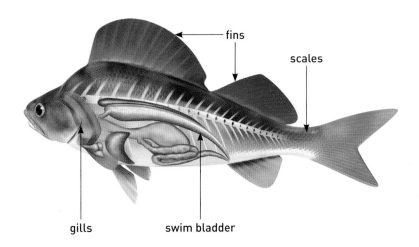

Fish have other special organs, too. Ninety-five per cent of fish are bony fish, and these fish all have a swim bladder. The swim bladder is like a bag of air, and it helps fish to move in the water. When the swim bladder takes in more air, the fish moves up in the water, and when the air goes out, it moves down.

Along each side of their body, most fish also have a special sense organ called the 'lateral-line system'. With this organ, fish can sense things moving in the water. So when fish see or hear a predator or prey nearby, they can feel it, too.

Sharks have a lateral-line system – but they also have another special sense which helps them to feel things. If you look closely at a shark's head, you can see several hundred little holes around its mouth. These are called the 'ampullae of Lorenzini', and they can sense the electrical signals which an animal makes when it moves a muscle. This means that a fish hiding under the sand is not safe from a shark: the shark's ampullae will sense even the very gentle moving of

the fish's gills.

With this special sense, it is not surprising that sharks, which also have excellent eyesight and smell, are the best predators among fish. So how can other fish keep safe from sharks and other powerful hunters?

Many fish stay deep in the sea during the day, and only come to the top to look for food at night, when there is less chance they will be seen. Other fish swim in a shoal – a group of lots of fish. When a group of fish are moving close together, and changing direction all at the same time, it is more difficult for a predator to catch them. So swimming in a shoal makes fish safer.

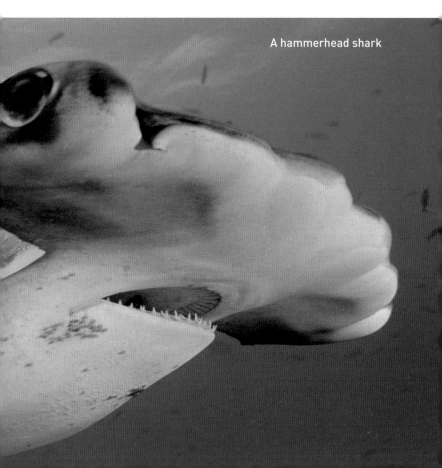

A hammerhead shark

A puffer fish

But the puffer fish can be very sure that no predator will want to eat it. When it is in danger, it changes itself quickly, taking in water or air, and makes its body two or three times bigger than usual. Soon, it is the shape of a ball, with long spines – so no animal can eat it.

Life in the water is dangerous for most fish, and for their young, it is very difficult to survive. Some sharks and other fish give birth to live young, but most fish lay eggs which are fertilized outside the female's body, and then hatch.

Because so few of their young survive, fish often lay a lot of eggs – sometimes as many as five million. Most fish leave their eggs when they have laid them or when they have fertilized them, but a few take great care of their young. Some species of cichlid fish keep their eggs or young in their mouths, where they are safe from predators and other dangers. They push water over the eggs to give them oxygen.

The sockeye salmon dies after breeding, and cannot care for its young – but it makes an extraordinary journey to lay its eggs. Most fish live in either fresh water or salt water, but the sockeye salmon moves from one to the other when it migrates to breed. After a life in the sea, it swims back up rivers to the place where it was born. Sockeye salmon make a journey of up to 2,500 km to return to their birth places, often jumping over rocks and dams to get there.

When they arrive, the females lay their eggs, which are fertilized by the males, and the adult salmon then die. The eggs hatch and the young salmon swim back the way their parents have come. Many will die on the long journey, but some will find their way to the sea, where they will stay until they are ready to breed themselves.

A sockeye salmon

6 Reptiles

Just as all birds have feathers, and all fish have wet scales, all reptiles have dry, scaly skin. But in other ways, many of the 9,500 different species of reptile are very different from each other.

There are four groups of reptiles. The largest reptile group – the squamata – includes four-legged lizards and snakes that are up to 15 m long. The chelonians – tortoises and turtles – are covered with a shell made of thin, hard plates. The alligators and crocodiles of the crocodilian group have long, strong tails and mouths full of teeth, and the smallest group, the tuataras, are like lizards but with three eyes when they are young. The third eye is on the top of their heads and can only be seen on baby tuataras.

Some reptiles are gentle, but others are among the most dangerous predators in the world. The reticulated python grows up to nearly 7 m long, and as well as eating mice, lizards, and frogs, a big one can also eat monkeys – and people. The python uses its one hundred sharp teeth to catch and bite its prey, and then puts its body around it, moving closer and closer until the animal cannot breathe. Then it eats the animal's body all at once.

The biggest lizard in the world is also a frightening predator, and it kills its prey in an interesting way, too. The Komodo dragon – which can grow to 3 m long – has a long, flat head, and a big, strong tail. It quietly waits until its prey comes near, and then attacks and bites it. The animal does

A Komodo dragon

not die immediately, but the bite makes it sick. The dragon follows its prey patiently until it cannot move – then it eats it.

Many snakes put poison into the bodies of their prey through sharp hollow teeth called fangs. Cobras have fangs at the front of their mouth. When a cobra is angry or frightened by another animal, it lifts its head up, pushes out the skin around it to make it look bigger, and then uses its fangs to shoot venom into the eyes of the animal. A cobra can attack from nearly 2 m away.

A cobra

Camouflage is very important for reptiles, to keep them safe from predators and to help them attack prey by surprise – and not many animals have better camouflage than the gaboon viper. With the brown shapes on its back, and its leaf-shaped head, this snake can hide among leaves on the floor of the forest. It waits there until it sees a rodent, bird, or frog, and then attacks.

The chameleon is also well-known for its clever camouflage. Different cells in its skin make different colours, so when the cells become bigger or smaller, it changes its body colour. Some chameleons change to be the same colour as the place around them. Chameleons also change colour to show other chameleons that they are angry, or ready to mate. The chameleon's colours also control how hot they are – dark colours take in heat, while light colours reflect it. In cold weather, a chameleon can make itself darker so its body is warm, and in warm weather, it can make itself lighter and cooler.

Camouflage is not the only clever feature of the chameleon. It also has special eyes, which can move in different directions at the same time – so one eye can watch the insect that it is hoping to catch, and the other eye can look out for predators. The chameleon is very fast, too, but often it does not have to chase prey. Instead, it uses its very long, sticky tongue to catch insects. The chameleon's tongue is as long as its body, and it can shoot it out very fast to catch prey.

A chameleon

An alligator with its young

Most reptiles lay eggs, and most do not care for their young when they hatch, but crocodilians are different. The female alligator builds a nest and stays near it when she has laid her eggs; then, when the young start to make noises, she pulls them from the nest, and helps them out of the eggs. She carries them carefully inside her mouth to the water.

Baby alligators stay near their mother for the first two years of their lives. They often need her help during this time, because they are in danger from many predators – including their own fathers.

Turtle parents are usually hundreds of kilometres away

when their young hatch from their eggs. Turtles migrate a very long way from the places where they live to their breeding places: some green turtles travel more than 3,000 km.

The turtles lay their eggs in the sand and then swim back home, so when their young hatch there is no one to protect them. The baby turtles find their way up out of the sand and then move down to the sea, but often birds and other predators are waiting for them. Some of the young turtles continue into the water and then begin the same journey their parents have already made. But only 1% of baby turtles survive to become adults.

7   Amphibians

A little tadpole swims along through the water in a lake, eating tiny plants. Its long tail pushes it forwards in the water, and it is breathing through gills on the side of its head. But only twelve weeks later, the tadpole will change into a very different kind of animal.

It will leave the lake that was its home and live on land, where it will stay until it is ready to breed. It will lose its tail, grow four legs, and start to breathe through lungs. And it will begin to eat spiders and other insects. The herbivorous tadpole from the lake will grow into a carnivorous frog that lives on land. Its body, and its way of living, will change completely, as it grows into an adult. This is called metamorphosis.

Amphibians are the only vertebrates in the animal kingdom that go through metamorphosis. Most of them live

A tadpole

A frog

for part of their lives in water (as young called larvae) and for part of their lives on land.

But not all amphibians go through these great changes. Young newts and salamanders look very like the adults. Many species of salamander live on land all through their lives, and others never leave the water.

There are three important groups of amphibians: frogs and toads; salamanders and newts (amphibians which look like lizards); and caecilians (amphibians which look like snakes and live underground).

Amphibians are ectothermic vertebrates, and they have smooth skin, with no hair or scales. Their skin is very special. Both water and oxygen can go through it, and most adult amphibians breathe through their skin as well as through their lungs. In fact, many adult amphibians breathe mostly through their skin, and only use their lungs when they are moving around a lot. Some amphibians almost never use their lungs, and some salamanders do not have lungs at all.

Amphibians can only breathe through their skin if it is wet, so they have something soft and sticky called mucus on it. Mucus stops their skin drying out. To help keep their skin wet, most amphibians also live near water. But some live in very hot, dry places – and they have clever ways of surviving there.

The water-holding frog lives in the hottest part of Australia. It takes in lots of water when it rains, and becomes up to 50% heavier than usual. Then it goes a metre under the ground, and its skin comes off and makes a kind of bag around the frog that keeps the water inside.
The frog then goes into a special kind of sleep, and does not move, eat, or drink for up to two years, until it rains again.

Like chameleons, many amphibians can change the colour of their skin. They can make it darker or lighter to keep themselves warm or cool.

A poison frog

Many amphibians have brightly-coloured skin, which they can use to frighten away predators. Poison frogs, which live in the rainforests of Central and South America, are bright yellow, red, blue, orange, and green. When predators see a frog's bright colours, they know that the frog is full of poison, and not safe to eat. The poison from one of these frogs can stop an animal from moving.

An amphibian can use its brightly-coloured skin to find a mate. When the great crested newt is ready to breed, the bottom of its body becomes bright orange, and it also grows a large crest down its back. A female will choose the newt with the biggest crest, because he will be a good mate.

A great crested newt

When most amphibians are ready to breed, they leave their homes on the land and go to the water. Some make long, difficult journeys back to the same lake or river year after year – sometimes to the place where they were born.

In most amphibian species, the females lay their eggs in the water, and the eggs are then fertilized by the males. Some amphibians lay only one or two eggs, but others lay up to fifty thousand. Amphibian eggs do not have a hard shell. They have a soft outer part, which protects them and stops them drying out. This part is often the first food for the larvae when they hatch.

But not all amphibians lay eggs. Some salamanders, like the black and yellow fire salamander, give birth to larvae. These larvae fight to stay alive – the fastest-growing young sometimes eat the smaller ones inside the mother's body.

For many amphibian larvae, the first few weeks of life are very dangerous. They are small, and cannot move fast or see well, so it is easy for predators to catch and eat them.

8   Invertebrates

Invertebrates are all around us: in the air above, in the grass under our feet, on the trees, and in the rivers and seas. In fact, when you are outside, you are probably never more than three metres away from one. Most are very small, and some are less than a millimetre long. We already know about more than one million species of invertebrate, but scientists think that there are many more.

Invertebrates are different from vertebrates because they have no bones and no backbone. There are many groups of invertebrate, and they are all very different. Some look like plants and do not move around; others are always moving. Some have tiny brains or no brain at all; others have a brain that is bigger than that of some vertebrates.

The biggest group of invertebrates is the arthropods. More than three out of four of the species of animal that we know about are arthropods, and the most important of these are insects, crustaceans, and arachnids.

Arthropods are very important in the food chain. They are what many birds, reptiles, fish, and most other animals eat. The blue whale, the biggest animal in the world, eats arthropods, too. Arthropods are also important because they break down dead plants and animals and move pollen from one plant to another.

A small, green shell hangs from the branch of a tree. Two days later, the shell becomes clear, and something colourful can be seen inside.

Metamorphosis: from caterpillar to butterfly

Slowly, the shell breaks open, and out comes a tiny orange and black butterfly. Its wings are small and wet, but they soon dry and become bigger. For an hour, the butterfly stays hanging from the shell, growing and growing – and then it flies away. In a week, it will mate and lay eggs which will hatch into tiny caterpillars. But only two weeks earlier, the butterfly was a caterpillar itself, hanging from the branch of the tree and ready to begin its amazing metamorphosis.

Spiders are born as little spiders, looking just like their parents. But many other arthropods, like the butterfly, begin life as larvae and change by metamorphosis into adults with wings. For some, like the dragonfly, the changes are a little slower. The young dragonfly, called a nymph, loses its skin several times as it grows. It then climbs out of the water, loses its skin for the last time, and becomes a dragonfly with beautiful long wings.

A dragonfly

A bee colony

Some arthropods live in big groups called colonies. They work together to get food, protect themselves, and breed. Bees are well-known for living like this. In every bee colony, there are tens of thousands of bees living together. Female worker bees collect pollen, clean, and take care of any young. There is also one queen bee, who lays eggs, and lots of male bees called drones, who mate with the queen.

The arthropods are amazing – but some of the animals in the other invertebrate groups are much simpler. The simplest of all living animals are the sponges. Most of the eight thousand species of sponge that we know about live in the sea, and they look like plants and do not move. They eat by filter feeding – water is taken in through thousands of holes in their bodies. They take oxygen and tiny bits of food from the water, and the water then moves back out of their body.

Another group of invertebrates, cnidarians, are filter feeders, too. But they also have an important feature that helps them to catch live prey: around their mouth they have tentacles with cells on them that sting.

One of the best known cnidarians is the jellyfish, which is found in every sea in the world. It has no brain, and is 98% water, but it can sting, and two species of jellyfish can kill people.

Echinoderms, the next important group of invertebrates, have a clever way of staying safe from predators. All echinoderms have five parts that go out from their middle, and the best-known animals in this group are starfish.

When a predator takes the arm of a starfish, the starfish can drop its arm – and then grow a new one. These amazing animals have an interesting way of eating, too. Because their mouths are very small, they push their stomachs out through their mouths, eat the prey that they have caught in their arms, and then pull their stomachs back into their body again.

Many invertebrate eggs and young do not survive, and become food for other animals, so invertebrates usually lay a lot of eggs. A starfish can lay two and a half million eggs in only two hours.

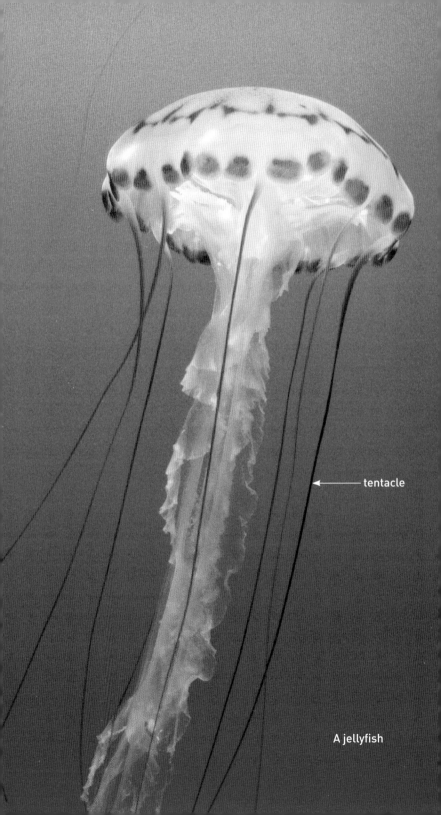

tentacle

A jellyfish

Many invertebrates do not care for their eggs or young, but the female octopus does. While she waits for her eggs to hatch, she pushes water over them to keep them clean, and protects them from predators. She does not eat while she is caring for her eggs, and dies after they have hatched. Although she works so hard, only one in every hundred baby octopuses survives.

The octopus is a mollusc – another important kind of invertebrate. Molluscs come in many different shapes, but they have a soft body, and most still have the hard shell that covered all molluscs millions of years ago.

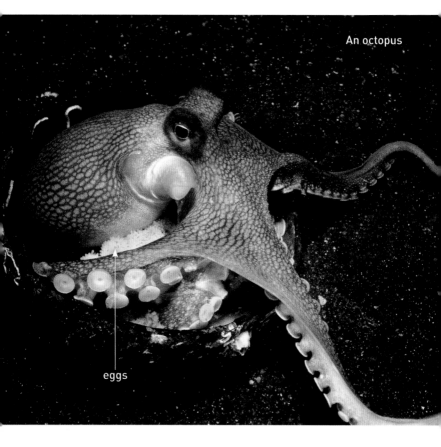

An octopus

eggs

A picture of a
giant squid

The biggest of all the molluscs is the giant squid, but because it lives at the bottom of the sea, it is not often seen. The giant squid has the biggest eyes in the animal kingdom – 20 cm across – and these help it to see in deep water, so it can easily find prey. It has long tentacles, too, so it can reach out up to 10 m away for animals that it wants to eat. The giant squid also has a clever way of staying safe from predators. When it feels in danger, it shoots a dark black colour into the water around it. Then, while the predator tries to understand what is happening, it escapes.

9 The future

Crash! Another tree falls to the ground – one of six thousand that are cut down every hour around the world. This one is cut down by people who are building a new farm. They are going to grow palm oil, which is useful for food and fuel. People who live near the farm will be able to work on it, and make money. That is good for everyone, surely?

No – not for the animals living in the rainforest. Many will die when the trees are cut down. But that is not the only problem that the farm will bring. For some species of rainforest bird, which do not like to move across open places, the farm will change the way they migrate. The farm will also break up the land that some animals move around in, so it will be more difficult for them to find food. And with less rainforest, there is less space for animals' habitats.

Cutting down too many trees is just one of the many problems people bring for animals. A hundred years ago, there were fewer than two billion people in the world; now there are more than seven billion. People need more space for living and farming, so forest, grassland, and wetlands are destroyed, water is taken from rivers and lakes, and animals lose the places where they live, breed, and find food.

Another problem people have introduced into the animal kingdom is pollution. Pollution happens when dirty and dangerous things that people have made get into the places where animals live and eat. As well as killing some animals, pollution can bring health problems to others, for example making it difficult for them to breed.

This is not the only kind of pollution that is making life difficult for animals. When fuels are burned, the air and rain become polluted, which is dangerous for fish and for many other animals. Air pollution also brings climate change, which is a danger to almost every animal species in the world.

An African elephant

Animals can evolve when the climate changes slowly, but the changes that are happening in the world now are coming too fast. The Earth and the seas are getting warmer, there is more water in the sea, and droughts (times when there is no rain) are getting longer and harder – and animals cannot evolve quickly enough to survive.

For the 3,200 wild tigers now left alive, and for other animals like rhinos and elephants, there is an even greater danger. Although there are laws to protect these beautiful animals, poachers still kill them for their skins and for their body parts.

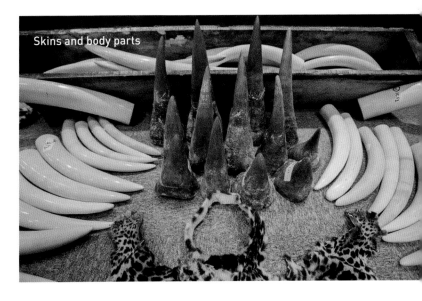

Skins and body parts

Too much fishing and hunting has destroyed large numbers of animal species, and some animals like turtles or seabirds are also caught by accident. There are now thousands of animal species in danger of becoming extinct: one in every four species of mammal, one in eight species of bird, and one third of all amphibians.

So what are we doing to make things better? There are now many organizations which work to try and keep animals safe. They make national parks and wildlife reserves, where no roads, factories, or houses are built, and where animals' natural habitats are protected. Captive breeding – catching animals and keeping them together to breed safely – has also stopped some animals from becoming extinct.

One example of this is the Californian condor. By 1987, there were only twenty-two condors left, because of hunting or pollution, or because many of their habitats had disappeared. So all the birds were caught for safe breeding, and twenty-five years later in 2012 there were over 400. Some of the condors were put back into their natural habitats again, and more than two hundred of them are now flying free in the wild.

Condor conservation

A Californian condor

People who work in conservation – saving animals and their habitats – want people to stop hunting wild animals, and to find other kinds of food. They are also telling people that when tourists come to see wild animals, it brings money to their villages and towns.

Other organizations are helping to protect the rainforests. They stop people cutting down lots of trees, and keep animals' habitats safe. Fishing equipment is changing, too, and many people are now using new equipment that will not catch animals like turtles and seabirds.

New laws and agreements between groups of countries have also helped to protect animals. Some of these agreements have stopped people moving animals from country to country, making it more difficult for them to sell animal skins or body parts. Other agreements have tried to stop people hunting animals that are in danger, like whales.

Countries and businesses are starting to come together to fight climate change, too, but this is still one of the biggest problems for the future of animals.

Darkness has come to the rainforest. Monkeys make their beds in the branches of the trees, and butterflies lie quietly under leaves, resting for the night. But other animals are just waking up. Bats fly through the air, looking for fruit, and flying frogs jump through the trees from branch to branch.

A tiger comes out, looking for food.

It is the end of another day in the rainforest – and hopefully just one of many for thousands of years to come, if we can protect these beautiful animals, and keep their habitats safe.

GLOSSARY

amazing *(adj)* If something is amazing, it surprises you very much and is difficult to believe.

attack *(v)* to start fighting or hurting somebody or something

backbone *(n)* the line of bones down the back of a body

bone *(n)* one of the hard white parts inside the body of a person or an animal

brain *(n)* the part inside the head of a person or an animal that thinks and feels

breathe *(v)* to take in and let out air through your nose and mouth

breed *(v)* When animals breed, they have young animals.

climate *(n)* the normal weather conditions of a place

communicate *(v)* to give information, ideas or feelings to another person or animal; **communication** *(n)*

direction *(n)* where a person, animal, or thing is going or looking

drought *(n)* a long time when there is not enough rain

equipment *(n)* special things that you need for doing something

extinct *(adj)* If a kind of animal or plant is extinct, it does not live now.

eyesight *(n)* the ability to see

feature *(n)* an important part of something

female *(adj)* an animal or person that can lay eggs or give birth to babies; opposite of male

fertilize *(v)* to put a seed in an egg, a plant, or a female animal and a baby, fruit or a young animal starts to grow; **fertilization** *(n)*

fuel *(n)* anything that you burn to make heat

give birth *(v)* to have a baby

hang *(v)* to fix something at the top (the lower part is free)

hatch *(v)* When baby birds, insects, or fish hatch, they come out of an egg.

hollow *(adj)* empty inside

hunt *(v)* to chase animals to kill them

hunter *(n)* a person who hunts wild animals

include *(v)* to have somebody or something as one part of
  the whole

insect *(n)* a very small animal that has six legs

law *(n)* a law says what people may or may not do in a country

lay *(v)* to make an egg

lungs *(n)* the parts in a body that are used for breathing

male *(adj)* A male animal or person does not have babies.

mate *(n)* one of two animals that come together to make young
  animals; *(v)* When animals mate, they come together to make
  young animals.

muscle *(n)* one of the parts inside a person or animal which help
  them to move

nest *(n)* a place where a bird, snake, insect, etc. keeps its eggs or
  its babies

organ *(n)* a part of your body that does something special, for
  example, a heart

organization *(n)* a group of people who work together for a
  special reason

oxygen *(n)* Oxygen is in the air. Animals and plants need oxygen
  to live.

poison *(n)* something that will kill you or make you very ill if
  you eat or drink it; *(v)* to use poison to kill or hurt someone
  or something

pollen *(n)* the yellow powder in flowers. Insects or the wind take
  it to other flowers.

powerful *(adj)* having a lot of strength

prey *(n)* an animal or bird that another animal or bird kills for
  food

protect *(v)* to keep somebody or something safe

rainforest *(n)* a forest in a hot part of the world where there is a
  lot of rain

reflect *(v)* to send back light, heat, or sound

sand *(n)* powder made of very small pieces of rock, that you find on beaches and in deserts

scientist *(n)* a person who studies science or works with science

sharp *(adj)* with an edge or point that cuts or makes holes easily

shell *(n)* the hard outside part of birds' eggs and nuts, and of some animals

signal *(n)* a light, sound, or movement that tells you something without words

simple *(adj)* without a lot of different parts or extra things

smooth *(adj)* having a very flat surface

sticky *(adj)* able to fix to things

sting *(v)* If an insect or a plant stings you, it hurts you by pushing a sharp part into your skin.

survive *(v)* to continue to live in or after a difficult or dangerous time

temperature *(n)* how hot or cold a thing or a place is

tiny *(adj)* very small

venom *(n)* poison that some snakes, spiders, etc. make when they bite or sting

wild *(adj)* Wild plants and animals live or grow in nature, not with people.

SOME NATURAL HABITATS

marine habitats water containing salt, like the sea

fresh water habitats water not containing salt, like rivers and lakes

terrestrial habitats places on land where animals live, for example:

desert a large, dry area of land with very few plants

forest a large area of land covered with trees

grassland a large area of open land covered with wild grass

polar near the top or bottom of the Earth (called the North Pole and the South Pole)

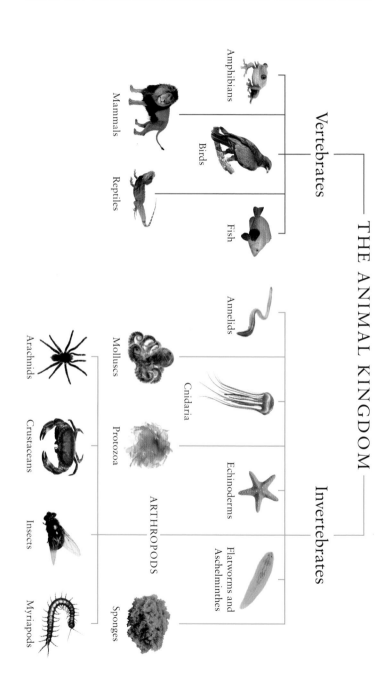

THE ANIMAL KINGDOM

Vertebrates

Amphibians

Mammals

Birds

Reptiles

Fish

Invertebrates

Annelids

Molluscs

Cnidaria

Protozoa

Echinoderms

Arachnids

Crustaceans

Insects

ARTHROPODS

Flatworms and
Aschelminthes

Myriapods

Sponges

ACTIVITIES

Before Reading

1 **Match the words below to the pictures.**

feathers / fin / gill / nest / shell / wing

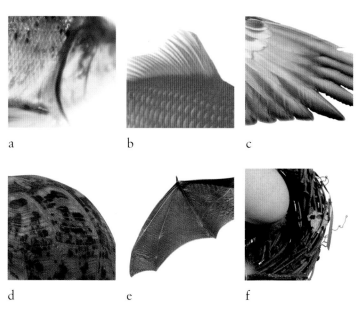

a   b   c

d   e   f

2 **Two of these sentences are true. Which ones?**

1 You can find animals everywhere on Earth. ☐
2 All animals have bones in their bodies. ☐
3 Scientists know fewer animal species now
   than they did a hundred years ago. ☐
4 All animals survive by eating other animals. ☐
5 Species change over time to match the place they live. ☐

ACTIVITIES

While Reading

Read Chapter 1. Then complete the sentences with the words below.

carnivores / cells / invertebrates / omnivores / species

1 Animals and plants are made of very small living things called _____ .
2 Animals which eat only meat are called _____ .
3 _____ can eat meat and plants.
4 _____ are animals that have no backbones.
5 A(n) _____ is the smallest group of animals that are the same.

Read Chapter 2. Then match the animals below to the descriptions.

bat / beaver / elephant / giraffe / mouse / snake

This animal …
1 can smell with its tongue. _____
2 builds a dam and lives behind it. _____
3 is born two years after fertilization. _____
4 only lives for about two years. _____
5 uses sound to sense the world around it. _____
6 became taller, perhaps to help it find food. _____

Read Chapter 3. Then find words in the chapter to complete these sentences.

1 Sixty-five million years ago, mammals were very _____ animals.

2 The placenta is an organ which gives a mammal food and _____ before it is born.

3 Baby mammals do not need to find food because their mothers can make _____ .

4 Mammals can live in very cold places because they have got _____ blood.

5 In winter, some mammals _____ for a few months.

Read Chapter 4. Then choose the correct answers.

1 Which feathers do birds use to fly?
   a) soft feathers   b) hard feathers

2 What is preening?
   a) cleaning feathers   b) making a nest

3 How far do Arctic Terns migrate?
   a) hundreds of kilometres   b) thousands of kilometres

4 What can all female birds do?
   a) lay eggs b) fly

5 What do birds of prey eat?
   a) animals b) fruit

6 Where do woodpeckers live?
   a) on water   b) in trees

Read Chapter 5. Then choose the correct words to complete the sentences.

1 Fish are the *oldest* / *newest* group of vertebrates.
2 Their bodies are *warmer than* / *as warm as* the water around them.
3 Fish use special organs called *gills* / *scales* to breathe.
4 The swim bladder helps fish to *sense things* / *move up and down*.
5 Sharks have got amazing senses of smell and *hearing* / *sight*.

Read Chapter 6. Then complete the sentences with animals from the book.

1 _____ and _____ have got hard shells.
2 _____ babies have got a third eye.
3 _____ can grow up to 7 m long.
4 _____ and _____ have got a very dangerous bite.
5 _____ can change their colour.
6 _____ look after their babies for two years.

Read Chapter 7. Then rewrite these incorrect sentences to make them true. Change one word only. Use the words below.

body / easy / ground / many / skin

1 Metamorphosis is when an animal changes its colour.
2 Many adult amphibians breathe through their gills.
3 All amphibians can change colour.
4 The water-holding frog spends most of its life under the water.
5 It is difficult for predators to catch amphibian larvae.

Read Chapter 8. Then find words in the chapter to complete these sentences.

1 You are probably never more than three metres away from an _____ .
2 A _____ changes into a butterfly.
3 Only the _____ bee lays eggs.
4 _____ feeders take in food and water through holes in their bodies.
5 Most molluscs have got hard _____ .

Read Chapter 9. Then complete the text with the words below.

habitats / farming / climate / hunting / cut down

Around the world, people (1) _____ thousands of trees every hour to make space for living and (2) _____ . But this destroys animals' (3) _____ . Fishing and (4) _____ kill a lot of animals, too, and pollution is changing the world's (5) _____ .

After Reading

Vocabulary

1 Match the adjectives to the definitions.

1 amazing
2 extinct
3 hollow
4 sharp
5 smooth
6 sticky
7 tiny

a cuts or makes holes easily
b empty inside
c surprises you very much
d very small
e having a very flat surface
f able to fix to things
g does not live now

2 Complete the sentences with the words below.

lungs / scales / lay / sense / fangs / mate

1 Birds have brightly coloured feathers to attract a _____ .
2 Mammals use their _____ to get oxygen.
3 Some fish _____ thousands of eggs.
4 Venomous snakes like the cobra have big _____ at the front of their mouth.
5 Many animals have an excellent _____ of smell.
6 Fish are covered in _____ to protect them.

Grammar

1 Match the sentence halves.

1 Snakes use an organ in their mouths …
2 Mammals need a lot of food …
3 Many birds migrate …
4 Some male birds sing or do dances …
5 Some animals use camouflage …
6 Some frogs are brightly coloured …

a … to smell things.
b … to hide from predators.
c … to find food in winter.
d … to keep their bodies warm.
e … to scare away predators.
f … to find a female.

2 Choose the correct quantifiers to complete the sentences.

1 *A lot of / A few* animal species are now in danger of becoming extinct.
2 *Some / All* mammals hibernate in the winter.
3 *A little / A few* species of birds cannot fly.
4 Only *a few / a little* of a fish's young survive.
5 *Many / Much* amphibians use their skin to breathe.

Reading

1 Find animals in the book which…

1 … can use poison to kill their prey.
2 … can change colour.
3 … change their bodies in their life cycle through metamorphosis.
4 … live in large groups.
5 … have warm blood.
6 … have hard shells to protect them.

2 Complete the sentences with the numbers below. Then check your answers in the book.

7 / 8 / 30 / 75 / 2,500 / 3,200 / 9,500 / 70,000

1 The blue whale can be _____ m long.
2 The peregrine falcon's eyes are _____ times better than human eyes.
3 The Arctic tern flies _____ km every year.
4 Sockeye salmon can swim up to _____ km to breed.
5 There are about _____ different species of reptile.
6 More than _____ % of all animals are arthropods.
7 There are more than _____ billion people on Earth today.
8 There are _____ tigers left in the world.

Writing

1 Read the factfile and answer the questions.

Factfile: fish

 Fish live in rivers, lakes, and seas all around the world. Fish are ectothermic – they have cold blood, so they are the same temperature as the water around them. Special organs called gills take oxygen out of the water so that fish can breathe. Fish use their fins to swim, and some fish can swim a very long way. The sockeye salmon swims up to 2,500 km to lay its eggs!

---

1 How can fish breathe under the water?
2 How do fish swim, and how far?

2 Use the notes to write a factfile about birds.

Factfile: birds

- 10,000 species, all over the world, from the Arctic to the rainforest
- warm blood, hollow bones, feathers
- all birds lay eggs, babies hatch
- most can fly, the world's fastest animal: peregrine falcon (300 km per hour)

---

3 Now write a factfile about mammals, reptiles, amphibians, or arthropods in your own words.

Speaking

1 Complete the sentences with the phrases below. Then underline the words used to give reasons or results.

they fall down / we do not usually see them /
their mothers produce milk / species can survive when
their habitat changes / animals are losing their habitats

1 People cut down trees so _____ .
2 Because invertebrates are tiny, _____ .
3 Because of evolution, _____ .
4 Beavers bite through trees, so _____ .
5 Young mammals do not have to look for food because

_____ .

2 Find the answers to these questions in the book.

1 Why do beavers build homes with water all around them? (Chapter 2)
2 Why do birds have feathers? (Chapter 4)
3 Why do fish lay a lot of eggs? (Chapter 5)
4 Why are arthropods so important for the food chain? (Chapter 8)

3 With a partner, discuss these questions.

1 Why are people cutting down a lot of trees?
2 Why do people hunt animals like rhinos and tigers?
3 Do you think the future will be better or worse for animals?

INDEX

A

agreements 55
alligators 32, 36–37
amphibians 38–41
ampullae of Lorenzini 28
Arctic terns 20
arthropods 42–45

B

bats 9
bears 17
beavers 10–11
bees 45
big cats 5
birds 18–25
birds of prey 19–20, 23
birdsong 20, 25
breathing 27, 38–39
butterflies 9, 42–44

C

caecilians 39
Californian condors 54–55
camouflage 18, 34–35
captive breeding 54
caring for young 13–15, 30,
  36–37, 45, 48
carnivores 3
catching prey 3, 23, 32–34,
  46, 49
chameleons 34–35
cheetahs 3, 13–14
chelonians 32, 36–37
cichlid fish 30
climate change 51, 53, 55
cnidarians 46–47
cobras 33

[continued]

colonies 45
colours 18, 20, 34–35, 40
communication 10
conservation 54–55
crocodiles 32
crocodilians 32, 36–37

D

danger 30, 46, 49
dragonflies 44

E

echinoderms 46
ectothermic animals 16, 27, 39
egg laying 14, 20, 30–31,
  36–37, 41, 44–46
egg tooth 20
eggs 7, 20, 30, 36–37, 41, 46,
  48
elephants 52
endothermic animals 16, 18
evolution 11, 13, 19, 53
extinction 53
eyes 32, 34–35, 49
eyesight 23, 29

F

fangs 33
feathers 18–20
fins 26–27
fish 26–31
fishing 53, 55
flamingos 24
flying 19–20
food 1, 3, 16, 20, 23–24, 28,
  33, 42, 46
food chain 2, 23, 42
frogs 7, 38–40

G

gaboon vipers 34
giant squid 49
gills 27, 38
giraffes 11–12
gizzard 20
great crested newt 40–41
groups 4–5, 14, 23, 32, 39

H

hair 15
heat 16, 18, 34, 39–40
herbivores 3
hibernation 16–17
homes 10
human population 51
hunting 53–55

I

invertebrates 4, 42–49

J

Jacobson's organ 9
jellyfish 46–47

K

kangaroos 15
kinds of animals 1
kiwis 19
Komodo dragons 32–33

L

lateral-line system 28
laws 53, 55
life cycles 6–7, 42–44
lions 5, 8
lizards 32, 34–35

M

mammals 13–17
marsupials 14–15
mating 7, 10, 20, 22, 40
metamorphosis 38, 42–44

mice 6
migration 20, 31, 37
milk 15
molluscs 48–49
monotremes 14
movement 8
mucus 39
muscles 8, 19–20

N

national parks 54
nests 20, 22, 36
newts 39–41

O

octopuses 48
omnivores 3
owls 23

P

passerines 25
peregrine falcons 19–20, 23
placental mammals 14
poaching 53
poison frogs 40
pollution 51
predators 3, 29, 33, 36–37, 41
preening 19
ptarmigan 18
puffer fish 30
pythons 2, 32–33

R

rainforests 1, 40, 50, 55–57
reptiles 13, 19, 32–37

S

safety 8, 10, 29, 46, 49
salamanders 39, 41
Satin Bowerbirds 22
scales 26–27
scents 10

senses 9, 28–29
sharks 28–29
shoals 29
sizes of animals 1
skin 18, 26, 32, 34, 39, 40, 44
snakes 1–2, 9, 33
sockeye salmon 31
species 4, 11
spiders 44
sponges 46
squamata 32–33, 35
starfish 46
survival 6–11
survival rates 30, 37, 41, 46, 48
swim bladder 27

T
tadpoles 38
teeth 32–33
tigers 53, 56–57
toads 39

tortoises 32
toucans 20–21
tourism 55
trees, cutting down 50–51
tuataras 32
turtles 32, 36–37

V
venom 33
vertebrates 4
see also amphibians; birds;
    fish; mammals; reptiles

W
waders 24
water-holding frogs 39–40
weaver birds 22
whales 1, 16–17
wildlife reserves 54
woodpeckers 25

Z
zebras 3

THE OXFORD BOOKWORMS LIBRARY

THE OXFORD BOOKWORMS LIBRARY is a best-selling series of graded readers which provides authentic and enjoyable reading in English. It includes a wide range of original and adapted texts: classic and modern fiction, non-fiction, and plays. There are more than 250 Bookworms to choose from, in seven carefully graded language stages that go from beginner to advanced level.

Each Bookworms Factfile has full colour photographs, and offers extensive support, including:

▸ extra support pages, including a glossary of above-level words
▸ activities to develop language and communication skills
▸ a complete audio recording
▸ online tests

Each Bookworm pack contains a reader and audio.

4	**STAGE 4**	▸ 1400 HEADWORDS	▸ CEFR B1–B2
3	**STAGE 3**	▸ 1000 HEADWORDS	▸ CEFR B1
2	**STAGE 2**	▸ 700 HEADWORDS	▸ CEFR A2–B1
1	**STAGE 1**	▸ 400 HEADWORDS	▸ CEFR A1–A2
S	**STARTER**	▸ 250 HEADWORDS	▸ CEFR A1

Find a full list of *Bookworms* and resources at
www.oup.com/elt/gradedreaders

If you liked this stage 3 Factfile, why not try...

Dinosaurs
TIM VICARY

Imagine an animal with teeth as big as bananas – and a brain as big as an orange. Or a flying animal with wings as wide as a small plane. Is it any surprise that people are interested in dinosaurs?